Heroes OF THE American Revolution

by Joe Adair

PEARSON

Scott Foresman

Editorial Offices: Glenview, Illinois • Parsippany, New Jersey • New York, New York
Sales Offices: Needham, Massachusetts • Duluth, Georgia • Glenview, Illinois
Coppell, Texas • Ontario, California • Mesa, Arizona

ISBN: 0-328-13311-6

7 8 9 10 V010 14 13 12 11 10 09 08

The Thirteen Colonies

In 1775 **America** did not have states. Instead, America had thirteen colonies. These colonies were ruled by a country called Great Britain. Great Britain was far away. Great Britain's king did not know what the colonies were like.

Original
13 Colonies
(now states)

ATLANTIC
OCEAN

America was very different in 1775. There were only thirteen colonies.

In 1775 trouble started between Great Britain and the Thirteen Colonies. Great Britain was taking tax money from the Colonies. The colonists did not want to pay this money. There were other problems too. The American Revolution began.

Colonists got angry at unfair British taxes.

Many Americans wanted to be independent from Great Britain. They were willing to fight for their **freedom**. Everyone who fought to make America free was a hero. But there were some special people worth remembering.

Benjamin Franklin

Benjamin Franklin was born in Boston in 1706. He wrote books and invented useful things. He invented the first swim fins. He also invented special glasses to help people see better. Benjamin Franklin also studied science. His work helped people understand how lightning and electricity work.

Franklin experimented with electricity.

During the American Revolution, Benjamin Franklin was sent to Europe. He asked France to help the colonists. He asked for guns for the American army. Benjamin Franklin spent many years helping to win the war against Great Britain. He worked to make America free. He is a hero of the American Revolution.

Benjamin Franklin is cheered as a hero.

George Washington

George Washington was born in Virginia in 1732. He is known as the "father of our country." He became the first President of the United States. Before he was President, George Washington was in charge of the army during the American Revolution.

A statue of the first President of the United States

The war was not easy. George Washington and his troops faced two very hard winters. They were very cold. They did not have enough food. George Washington did not let his troops give up. He fought hard to help America win the war against Britain.

American troops cross the Delaware River.

The last really big battle of the American Revolution is called the Battle of Yorktown. French soldiers and sailors helped the Americans in this battle. On October 19, 1781, the Bristish soldiers gave up and asked for the war to end. George Washington was a very smart general. He is remembered as a hero of the American Revolution.

George Washington led Americans to victory.

Some Surprising Heroes

You may be surprised to know that women, and even some children, fought in the American Revolution. A woman named Deborah Sampson wanted to join the fight for freedom. She dressed like a soldier and joined the army. She fought in many battles. She later wrote about her experiences during the war.

Deborah Sampson dressed as a soldier during the American Revolution

Margaret Corbin went to war with her husband, John. John Corbin was in charge of a cannon. When John was shot during a battle, Margaret quickly took his place. She continued to fire the cannon until she was wounded too. Margaret Corbin was later honored by the new United States government.

Women fought during the American Revolution.

Sybil Ludington was a hero at 16. She rode her horse all night to call American soldiers together to save her burning town.

Dicey Langston earned the **nickname** "Daring Dicey." When she was just 15, she heard British soldiers planning an attack. She walked all night and crossed a wide river to warn the Americans.

This statue honors Sybil Ludington and her daring ride. The stick in her hand was the only protection she had.

The Flag and the Fourth

During the American Revolution, the first **flag** of the new America was made. This flag had thirteen **stars** for the thirteen colonies. Today, the American flag has fifty stars and thirteen **stripes**. The stars stand for the fifty states. The stripes stand for the thirteen colonies of the past.

On the original American flag, there were 13 stars, one for each of the 13 colonies.